Words by Anna McQuinn • Pictures by Ruth Hearson

ZEKi RISE AND SHINE

Alanna Max

Zeki has had a big sleep. Now it is time to wake up to a new day.

With a swish,
the lemon-yellow sun
sparkles in.

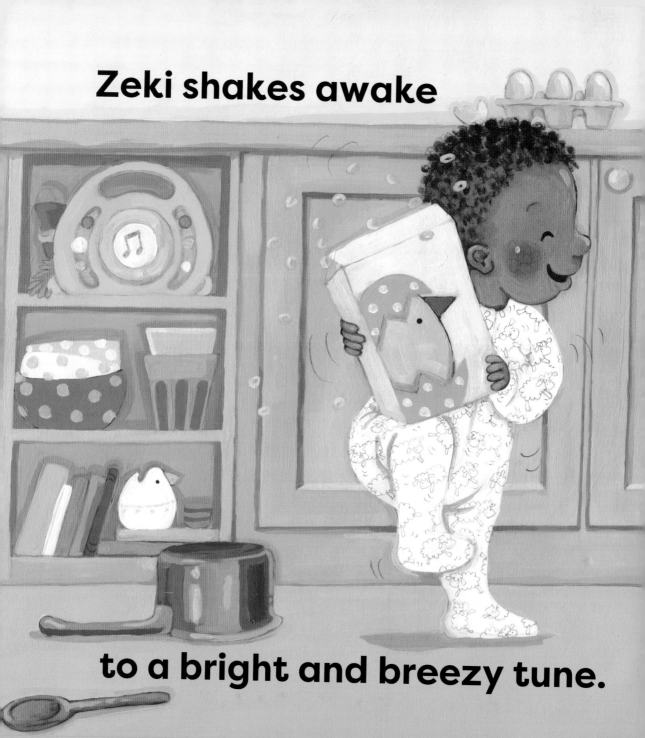

Zeki shakes awake

to a bright and breezy tune.

He munches on crunchies.
He sips zingy juice.

A quick splash
and Zeki is
minty fresh.

Bippity bop!

A buzzy top
for a busy bee.

Bounce and groove!

Zeki shimmies
into sharp shorts.

Heel, toe –
yellow jellies...

for happy feet!

Zeki is wide awake
and ready for anything!

For Priscilla – A.McQ

For Elodie – R.H.

Scan the QR code to visit the Activities
and Resources page on our website.

Published in the UK & Ireland by Alanna Max
Zeki Rise and Shine © 2022 Alanna Max
Text copyright © 2022 Anna McQuinn
Illustrations copyright © 2022 Ruth Hearson
Zeki Rise and Shine is part of the Zeki Books series developed
by and published under licence from Anna McQuinn
www.AnnaMcQuinn.com
All Rights Reserved
www.AlannaMax.com
Printed in China
ISBN 978-1-907825-43-9
23456789